Introducing Continents

Africa

Chris Oxlade

Raintree is an imprint of Capstone Global Library Limited, a company incorporated in England and Wales having its registered office at 7 Pilgrim Street, London, EC4V 6LB – Registered company number: 6695582

To contact Raintree, please phone 0845 6044371, fax + 44 (0) 1865 312263, or email myorders@ raintreepublishers.co.uk.

Text © Capstone Global Library Limited 2014
First published in hardback in 2014
The moral rights of the proprietor have been asserted.

Edited by Dan Nunn, Rebecca Rissman, Sian Smith, and Helen Cox Cannons
Designed by Philippa Jenkins
Original illustrations © Capstone Global Library Ltd 2014
Picture research by Liz Alexander and Tristan Leverett
Production by Vicki Fitzgerald
Originated by Capstone Global Library Ltd
Printed and bound in China by Leo Paper Products Ltd

ISBN 978 1 406 26292 6
17 16 15 14 13
10 9 8 7 6 5 4 3 2 1

British Library Cataloguing in Publication Data
Oxlade, Chris
Introducing Africa. – (Introducing continents)
A full catalogue record for this book is available from the British Library.

Acknowledgements
We would like to thank the following for permission to reproduce photographs: Alamy pp. 19 (© imagebroker); Corbis pp. 18 (© Andrew Aitchison/In Pictures), 26 (© George Steinmetz); Getty Images pp. 11 (Nigel Pavitt/AWL Images), 16 (Mint Images - Frans Lanting), 27 (Issouf Sanogo/AFP); naturepl.com p. 15 (© Nick Garbutt); Shutterstock pp. 6 (© N Mrtgh), 7 (© Przemyslaw Skibinski), 8 (© ricardomiguel.pt), 9 (© Graeme Shannon), 10 (© bumihills), 12 (© POZZO DI BORGO Thomas), 13 (© Vadim Petrakov), 14 (© Eric Isselee), 17 (© Rechitan Sorin), 21 (© Wessel du Plooy), 23 (© Frontpage), 24 (© Steve Heap), 25 (© urosr); SuperStock p.20 (Tips Images).

Cover photographs of Mt Kilimanjaro at sunrise, Massai Warriors in Tanzania, and shaded relief map of Africa all reproduced with permission of Shutterstock (© javarman, © Hector Conesa, © AridOcean).

Every effort has been made to contact copyright holders of material reproduced in this book. Any omissions will be rectified in subsequent printings if notice is given to the publisher.

Contents

Some words are shown in bold, **like this**. You can find out what they mean by looking in the glossary.

About Africa

Africa is one of the world's seven **continents**. A continent is a huge area of land. Africa is the second largest continent. Half of Africa is north of the **equator**, and half is south of the equator.

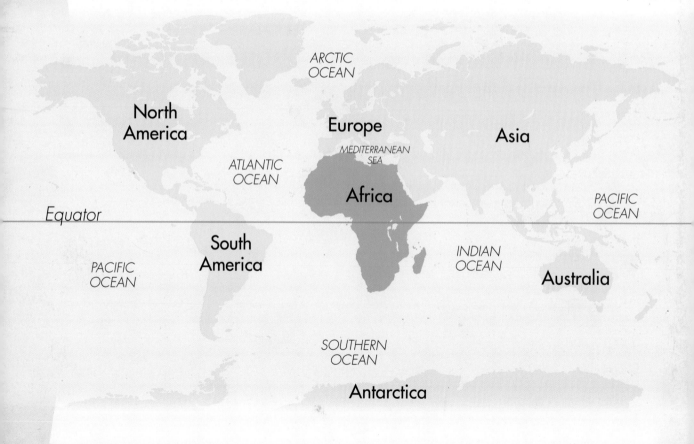

ARCTIC
OCEAN

North
America

Europe

Asia

MEDITERRANEAN
SEA

ATLANTIC
OCEAN

Africa

PACIFIC
OCEAN

Equator

South
America

INDIAN
OCEAN

PACIFIC
OCEAN

Australia

SOUTHERN
OCEAN

Antarctica

Africa is almost surrounded by sea. To the west is the Atlantic Ocean. To the east is the Indian Ocean. The Mediterranean Sea is to the north. The huge island of Madagascar is also part of Africa.

Africa fact file	
Area	About 30,365,000 square kilometres (11,724,000 square miles)
Population	1,051 million
Number of countries	56
Highest mountain	Kilimanjaro at 5,895 metres (19,341 feet)
Longest river	River Nile at 6,650 kilometres (4,132 miles)

Famous places

You might have heard of some of the famous places in Africa. Some of these places are ancient. The pyramids are in Egypt, near the city of Cairo. Ancient Egyptians built them about 4,500 years ago.

This photograph shows the Sphinx and the Great Pyramid.

The local name of the Victoria Falls is Mosi-oa-Tunya, which means "smoke that thunders".

The Victoria Falls are on the River Zambezi, between the countries of Zambia and Zimbabwe. They are 1,708 metres (5,604 feet) wide, and 99 metres (324 feet) high.

Geography

In the north and south of Africa are vast **deserts**, with huge sand dunes. The Sahara desert covers nearly the whole of North Africa. The Namib Desert and the Kalahari Desert are in the south.

The Sahara desert is the largest hot desert in the world.

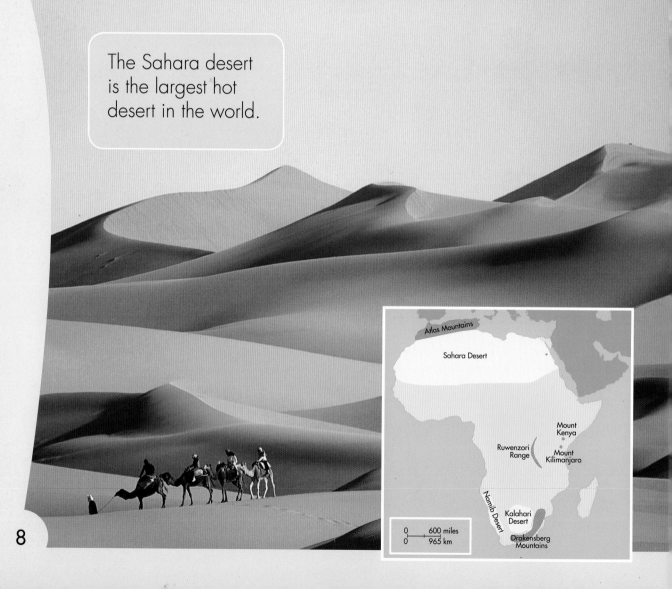

Atlas Mountains

Sahara Desert

Mount Kenya

Ruwenzori Range

Mount Kilimanjaro

Namib Desert

Kalahari Desert

Drakensberg Mountains

| 0 | 600 miles |
| 0 | 965 km |

Kilimanjaro is a **volcano** but it does not erupt any more.

There are vast grassy plains in Africa, called grasslands. Along the **equator** there are rainforests. Kilimanjaro and Mount Kenya are the two highest mountains in Africa. They are in East Africa.

The Nile is the longest river in the world. It starts in the middle of Africa and flows all the way to the Mediterranean Sea. Other great rivers in Africa are the Congo, Niger, and Zambezi.

The River Nile flows through the desert in Egypt.

These fishermen are preparing their boats on the shores of Lake Victoria.

Lake Victoria is the largest lake in Africa. It is also the second largest lake in the world. It measures 337 kilometres (209 miles) from north to south and 240 kilometres (149 miles) from west to east. More than 200 different types of fish live in the lake.

Weather

In much of Africa, the weather is warm or hot most of the time. Along the **equator**, the weather is **tropical**. It is hot and wet all year round. It rains nearly every day in the rainforests.

Trees and other plants grow well in the warm, wet tropical weather.

Heavy rain showers move across the African plains during the rainy season.

In the grasslands, there is a dry season, when it never rains, and a rainy season, when it rains almost every day. In the **deserts**, it is dry all year round. It is roasting hot in the daytime, but cold at night.

Animals

An amazing variety of animals live in Africa. Elephants, giraffes, rhinoceroses, and lions live on the grasslands. There are also big herds of zebra, wildebeest, and antelopes. Gorillas live in the rainforests.

Herds of wildebeest and elephants live on the African plains.

These ring-tailed lemurs live in a nature reserve in Madagascar.

Madagascar is a large island on the east coast of Africa. Most of the animals that live here don't live anywhere else on Earth. The most famous are the lemurs.

Plants

Many unusual plants grow in Africa. Plants grow very well in the wet, warm rainforests. There are huge trees, such as mahogany trees and ebony trees. There are also amazing plants, such as orchids and African violets.

These beautiful orchids are growing in the rainforest in Madagascar.

Palm trees grow in the desert where water comes up from underground.

Baobab trees with thick trunks and thorny acacia trees stand in the grasslands. Palm trees grow at **oases** in **deserts**. Papyrus grows along the banks of the River Nile. The ancient Egyptians used papyrus to write on like paper.

People

There are hundreds of different groups of people living in different parts of Africa. Big groups include Arabs and Berbers in North Africa. Some small groups of people, such as the Mbuti, live in the rainforests.

Mbuti pygmies live in the Democratic Republic of Congo. They hunt animals and gather plants.

Many different languages are spoken in Morocco, including Arabic, Berber and French.

More than 1,500 different languages are spoken in Africa. People have spoken these African languages for thousands of years. In many African countries, people also speak English, Portuguese, French, or Arabic.

African culture

Many African people still do their traditional dances on special occasions. They dress in traditional costumes and some wear body paint. Masai men in East Africa perform a special jumping dance.

These Chuka people from Kenya play traditional music on drums.

Most towns and villages in Africa have a dirt football pitch.

Football is the most popular sport in Africa. Every two years the national football teams of African countries play in the Africa Cup of Nations. Cricket is played in South Africa, Zimbabwe, and Kenya.

Countries

There are 56 countries in Africa. Algeria, in North Africa, is the largest. The Seychelles in the Indian Ocean is the smallest. It is made up of many islands.

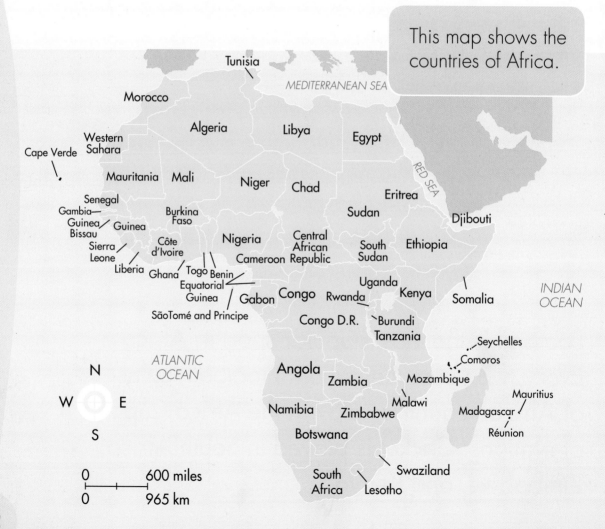

This map shows the countries of Africa.

Juba is the capital of South Sudan, which is Africa's newest country.

Countries from Europe once ruled most of Africa. That is why people in some African countries speak English or French. A new African country was made in 2011, when South Sudan split away from the rest of Sudan.

Cities and countryside

Four in every ten Africans live in a city. Cairo, the capital city of Egypt, is the African city with the greatest number of people. Eleven million people live here. Many people live in **slums**, without electricity or running water.

This is a view over the rooftops of Cairo, the capital of Egypt.

In many African villages, people get water from their village well.

In the countryside, people live in small villages. Many make a living from farming or by looking after herds of animals. Some also find food by hunting animals and gathering plants.

Natural resources and products

Africa has many **natural resources**. Oil is found under the ground in North Africa and West Africa. Nigeria produces the most oil of any country in Africa. Diamonds and gold are mined from the ground in South Africa.

These are oil wells on the banks of the Niger River, in Nigeria.

A farmer in the Ivory Coast cuts down pods full of cacao beans.

Farmers grow crops for themselves, to sell at market, or to send to other countries. Bananas, yams, coffee, tea, and peanuts are popular crops to grow. Most of the world's cacao beans come from West Africa. They are turned into chocolate.

Fun facts

- The Great Rift Valley is a huge valley in East Africa. It is 6,400 kilometres (4,000 miles) long and up to 100 kilometres (60 miles) wide.

- The Suez Canal carries huge ships 163 kilometres (101 miles) across the **desert** between the Red Sea and the Mediterranean Sea.

- A large amount of the world's gold comes from mines in South Africa.

- The cheetah lives on the grasslands of Africa. It can reach a speed of 113 kilometres (70 miles) per hour when it is chasing **prey**.

Quiz

1. Which African river is the longest river in the world?

2. Which city are the pyramids at Giza close to?

3. On which island do lemurs live?

4. What plant that grows in Africa does chocolate come from?

4. The cacao tree

3. Madagascar

2. Cairo, in Egypt

1. The Nile

Glossary

continent one of seven huge areas of land on Earth

desert area of land that gets very little rain

equator imaginary line running around the middle of Earth

natural resources natural materials that we use, such as wood, coal, oil, and rock

oases places in a desert where plants can grow because there is water just under the ground

prey animal that is hunted and eaten by another animal

slums overcrowded area of a city where poor people live

tropical place near the equator where the weather is hot and rainy all year

volcano mountain with a hole in the top which ash or hot melted rock comes out of

Find out more

Books

Africa (Exploring Continents), Deborah Underwood (Heinemann Library, 2008)

Horrible Geography of the World, Anita Ganeri (Scholastic, 2010)

Oxford First Atlas (OUP, 2010)

Websites to visit

kids.discovery.com/tell-me/people-and-places/our-7-continents
Various games, puzzles, and activities about the seven continents can be found on this website.

kids.nationalgeographic.com/kids/games/geographygames/copycat
This fun game helps you to find the continents on a map of the world.

www.worldatlas.com
This site has lots of maps, facts, and figures about continents.

Index